The Book of Tasks

Also by Christopher Spranger

The Effort to Fall
The Comedy of Agony: A Book of Poisonous Contemplations

THE BOOK of TASKS

Volume I: Atlantean Undertakings

Christopher Spranger

COYOTE ARTS

Albuquerque, New Mexico

The Book of Tasks. Volume I: Atlantean Undertakings. Copyright © 2022 Christopher Spranger.

All rights reserved. No part of this publication may be reproduced, stored in a retrieval system or transmitted in any form or by any means, electronic, mechanical, photocopying, recording or otherwise without the prior permission of the publisher.

Cover photograph: Atlas of the Marquis of Bendañaam, 1759, figure on the Museum Eugenio Granell, historic centre, Santiago de Compostela. imageBROKER / Alamy Stock Photo. Used by permission.

ISBN   978-1-878580-04-7 paper
           978-1-878580-05-4 e-book
LCCN   2020945381

Coyote Arts LLC
PO Box 6690
Albuquerque, New Mexico 87197-6690
coyote-arts.com

As carefully as if you were the insuperable enemy of your own unseen blindness read the book left unwritten hidden in the one now open in your hands.

Contents

Awaken	1
Discover Yourself	13
Translate the Silence of God	23
Attain the Truth	35
Practise the Highest Virtue	47
Generate Positivity	59
Become a Mirror of the Universe	71
Reach the Heights of Joy	81
Achieve Perfection	91
Rise Toward Heaven	101
Sit in the Center of a Circle of Light	115
Live Another Day	125

Awaken

I
Awaken confused.

II
Forget you have lived before.

III
Preserve the universe in that state of perfection you found it in unawares.

IV

All memory of the vast multitude of material forms of which you have been the somnolent tenant over the long and nebulous course of the last eighty-four thousand years having been blotted from your mind by amnesia obliviously enwomb yourself and be born yet again as if for the first time.

V

Admit you don't know why the moon is there.

VI

Every two and a half minutes recite the names of ten hundred thousand angels.

VII

Survive, henceforth, by consuming light alone, having lost your appetite for everything else.

VIII

Awaken without knowing yourself, or where you are, or that you are awake, in the simulacrum of a world your unconscious mind created without your awareness one night as you slept in a dream you failed to remember a single detail about on awaking the following day during a previous life you have also forgotten, one of innumerably many you have had, when you existed before as another man with another name and another face neither of which you would have the faintest chance of recognizing now.

IX

Forget the ground beneath you.

X

Occupy an indiscernible point.

XI

Bring what preceded the universe back.

XII

Become more delicately incandescent with each passing hour.

XIII

Sleepily prophesy a future like the past which has vanished in which you will obliviously live through everything that eludes your memory once again.

XIV

Celebrate the inscrutable character of the destiny you've been assigned.

XV

Untouched by life's trials let your tranquility exceed that of a stick of dynamite which has just exploded.

XVI

Leave a radiant stream of light in your wake as you walk out the door.

XVII

Your feet riveted to the earth, reach out across the stars.

XVIII

Trip over your physical body in a state of otherworldly ecstasy.

XIX

Evince such discretion in the saintliness you cultivate unconsciously that the stream of light you leave in your wake as you walk, of so supernaturally violent a radiance it should lacerate human eyes, is never noticed by anyone.

XX

Lose twenty-seven centuries of sleep in the space of a single night.

XXI

Catch the silence, before it can escape, in a net of closed eyelids.

XXII

Awaken in a paradise you don't perceive.

XXIII

Make listening to the silence of God your sole recreation.

XXIV

Repeatedly die in pursuit of the unnamable.

XXV

Entirely without meaning to kill in less than a minute everyone whose acquaintance you make with a smile whose supernatural radiance emanates outward with a violence you try in vain to suppress.

XXVI

Find the secret of deliverance in the failure to dream.

XXVII

Learn to love what you can't remember.

XXVIII

Say as slowly as perfect realization a prayer that saves everyone.

XXIX

Purify your to-do list of all that's superfluous by henceforth permitting nothing but miracles to appear there.

XXX

Live like today ended long ago.

XXXI

Repeatedly perish in the indefatigable pursuit of forever unreachable luminous spheres.

XXXII

Awaken in a paradise you don't perceive which, at the very moment you suspect it might be there, vanishes unnoticed.

XXXIII

Determined to achieve the magnitude which best accords with true modesty, shrink until you occupy an indiscernible point.

XXXIV

Act the same way now as you would in the perfect world.

XXXV

Come to a complete rest in perpetual collapse.

XXXVI

Fashion a boat of blazing rubies out of what's left of the sky after the sun explodes.

XXXVII

Live for one endless moment of emulated bliss.

XXXVIII

Tightly wrapped from head to toe in sheets of shimmering azure sneak unseen into the afternoon sky.

XXXIX

Cloak yourself in midnight's hidden colors.

XL

Awaken in a delirium of inverted realization one hour before dawn to paint inaccurate pictures of the afterworld on the kitchen floor with pancake syrup.

Discover Yourself

XLI

Discover yourself where you aren't, always the same.

XLII

Somehow dislodged from that indiscernible point of stillness where you belong in the vast ocean of vacancy that preceded the appearance of Being search in vain for the unborn version of yourself that's been lost.

XLIII

Start each day astonished to discover you still exist.

XLIV

Call out to the hour of your death silently from a distance.

XLV

With mist collected from the mountains an hour before dawn, draw your first memory in the air.

XLVI

Carve an image of your remotest ancestor into the face of a mountain while hanging upside down by your feet from a cloud.

XLVII

Commit suicide, yet quietly remain.

XLVIII

Pick up, with the fingers of your reflected image, the pieces of a shattered mirror.

XLIX
Permanently remain one minute behind the present moment.

L
Holding a brush of wind in your hand moving as fast as the wing of a hummingbird write the history of the world on the surface of a river about to flood its banks.

LI
Celebrate autumn by staying inside and staring at a picture of deciduous trees.

LII
Make a continual effort to forget what's gone until you realize nothing is.

LIII
Make a tomb of your mind.

LIV

Come to a complete rest in the perpetual collapse of all composite things.

LV

Oblivious to the blood coursing through your veins, take refuge in pure abstraction.

LVI

Become the shadow of a bird.

LVII

Glide along the ground, the dark, bodiless, disconnected shadow of both of a bird's wings with nothing between them but emptiness.

LVIII

Let your life go on without you.

LIX

Embrace the vanishing mirage of your own being.

LX

Abide undisturbed in the unseen essence of your singularity.

LXI

Withdraw in horror from what has already happened.

LXII

Do no more than remember nothing.

LXIII

Breathe in once again everything that has come back.

LXIV

Moving blindly away from yourself, smash into an empty mirror.

LXV

Populate your mind, in this moment, with precisely the same thoughts which used to appear there, day after day, in recurring fashion, fifteen to thirty years ago.

LXVI

Walk through a mile-thick wall of mist into a distant time you don't remember.

LXVII

Conspire with time's nonexistence to cancel the moment to come.

LXVIII

Follow the first road you see back to the beginning of the world.

LXIX

Fall, as if pushed by a crepuscular light, toward a cloudy reflection of paradise.

LXX

Float, as if your consciousness had come detached from time, outside the confines of past, present, and future, neither remembering what was nor experiencing what is nor anticipating what is to come.

LXXI

Be the one you have forgotten you are.

LXXII

Develop such a large constellation of opaque qualities you become difficult to perceive.

LXXIII

Become the mirror image of a self you've never seen.

Translate the Silence of God

LXXIV

Translate the silence of God through the agency of seven angels sounding seven trumpets in succession.

LXXV

Stand before yourself at the beginning of time.

LXXVI

Savor the divine sweetness of a world without substance.

LXXVII

Leap into an ocean of divine light from a mountain of bones in boots of stained glass the color of blood.

LXXVIII

Never become conscious of what you cannot annihilate.

LXXIX

Find your personal identity in the patterns on the floor.

LXXX

Install yourself in the kaleidoscopic vacuum of the self you have created.

LXXXI

Take a breath so deep you die halfway through it.

LXXXII

Reset the seasons with a cosmic sneeze.

LXXXIII

Relentlessly push everything backward, until it reaches its point of origin.

LXXXIV

Cut days from the calendar or tack them on, causing the years to swell or diminish according to your whim.

LXXXV

Come into this world without knowing why and quit it none the wiser.

LXXXVI

Chew off all the legs of the furniture in the living room with teeth like ten inch knives.

LXXXVII

Penetrate as deep into the ancient secrets of the night as the thinly painted façade of your sanity can endure.

LXXXVIII

Dig the translucent eyes of an angel of light out of the ashes of a silver castle of destroyed clouds.

LXXXIX

Indiscriminately welcome everything that comes.

XC

Split each moment of distracted consciousness you experience into seventy-four million distinct parts.

XCI

Increase the natural incandescence of your inescapable suffering.

XCII

Sleep henceforth as if your bed were a grave, the sound of your snores as full of serenity as what rots underground.

XCIII

Having closed your eyes to everything but your mind's picture of the afterworld leap arm in arm with an angel of light out of a hundred story window.

XCIV

Fall straight down from the sky.

XCV

Drive the shadow of love through a river of fire in reverse.

XCVI

Fold a triangular constellation of fallen stars into the disarray of a night come unwound, your fingers shaking with nervous exhaustion.

XCVII

Draw closer to the impossible through an act of prayer.

XCVIII

Watch the inconsolable weeping of the dead through a frosted window in your dream.

XCIX

Introduce a principle of fickleness and inconstancy into the calendar which provokes unpredictable derangements of periods previously fixed, thereby transforming this inflexible protector of routine into a liquid accomplice of the chaos it was created to prevent.

C

Stand on your head at the foot of a mountain blanketed with fog late one Wednesday morning.

CI

Conceive no end of superfluous designs.

CII

Interrupt a mechanical process at the critical moment without meaning to.

CIII

Live now in the same way as you would if everything in the world were to stop working at once.

CIV

Six minutes before you depart disprove everything that's been said.

CV

Frame with gold your favorite parts of the deadly struggle for prominence.

CVI

Using scissors of invisible light cut a horizontal series of triangular holes in the fabric of universal truth.

CVII

Seek to accomplish nothing for a reason not uniquely your own.

CVIII

Watch, speechless, as everything you considered solidest succumbs to the corrosive powers which have been relentlessly gnawing away at it and slips through your fingers like sand from a broken hourglass.

CIX

Breathe yourself back in time ten hundred thousand years.

CX

Be the light from above that arrives at the penultimate moment to consolingly immerse what little remains of a ruined world in its radiance.

CXI

Perceive the sudden departure of the silence you love.

Attain the Truth

CXII

Attain the truth, entirely unconscious.

CXIII

Wait, unseeing, at the entrance to what you are.

CXIV

Remain sufficiently confused to continue searching in vain.

CXV

Approach the place where words stop.

CXVI
Visualize the limit.

CXVII
Know now you need much less reality than you thought.

CXVIII
Write to confirm your unreserved commitment to what you are all but convinced is impossible.

CXIX
Disenchanted with forms and free of definitions renounce your muse and mine the void.

CXX
Reach the truth by erasing the path that leads to it.

CXXI

As soon as you find them immediately forget the answers you wasted your life looking for.

CXXII

Discover infinite serenity in the presence of a dead alphabet.

CXXIII

Be a fertile generator of indefinite conclusions.

CXXIV

Stay longer than you wish to with what you don't understand.

CXXV

Imagine you have just met Truth in the mind, impishly masquerading as rational thought.

CXXVI

Find meaning where none ever was.

CXXVII

Pray without words for what language is powerless to express.

CXXVIII

Notice time is running out.

CXXIX

Visualize the limit of delusion to which your own certainty can lead you.

CXXX

Provide a clear summary of what doesn't make sense.

CXXXI

Shove all the secrets of nature down the throat of your theoretical model.

CXXXII

Erase the dictionary, one word per day.

CXXXIII

Admit your best ideas were mistakes.

CXXXIV

Forget the surface exists.

CXXXV

Suffer unforeseen acts of treachery at the hands of multiple hidden meanings.

CXXXVI

Released from the reassuring chains the mind is forced to wear by rational thought pursue your fundamental bafflement with unprecedented zeal.

CXXXVII

Celebrate the indecipherable.

CXXXVIII

Study nothing but ancient inscriptions you've personally discovered.

CXXXIX

After splurging on a banquet of theological illusion, split the bill with your heavenly double.

CXL

Find what you seek in the essential opacity of what refuses to yield to analysis.

CXLI

Search for the source of corruption at the site of truth.

CXLII

Retreat in terror from mental clarity.

CXLIII

Seek to participate in the apparent nonexistence of what has not yet been named.

CXLIV

Emancipated from the mental effort thought requires meditate on what the mind is powerless to conceive.

CXLV

Know now you need reality much less than you thought.

CXLVI

Live without looking at yourself.

CXLVII

Having lost all sense of where you are, remain.

CXLVIII

Secure quietude by destroying wisdom.

CXLIX

Limit yourself to what's least perceptible about the object you wish to analyze.

CL

Discover a secret entrance to the sun in a sentence from a manuscript of which nothing survives.

CLI

Each morning, before you rise from bed, dismantle the structure of your mind.

CLII

Let every discovery you make lead you deeper into unknowing.

CLIII

Notice, once again, ignorant of what hour you have reached, time is running out.

CLIV

Having realized nothing is what it seems, refuse to investigate further.

Practise the Highest Virtue

CLV
Practise the highest virtue without comprehension.

CLVI
Die to the world, unaware you have.

CLVII
Repent with the utmost sincerity upon coming to recognize yourself as the one responsible for all the crimes others have been accused of.

CLVIII

By dint of the futile gestures you perform, benefit millions.

CLIX

Transform your heart into a secret treasury of impossible aspirations.

CLX

Fearlessly meet the gaze of unbridled malevolence as if immune to its vaporizing power.

CLXI

Do what cannot be accomplished out of a desire to attain what cannot be conceived.

CLXII

Manage your shadow with the singular diligence engendered by a sure method.

CLXIII

Cut an imperceptible path through a crowd of illustrious persons, nameless, unseen, content.

CLXIV

Win the favor of a faraway god of whose existence you will never become aware.

CLXV

Confirm how swiftly light travels through the sky as you sleep.

CLXVI

Perform miracles of delight separated from your mind.

CLXVII

Grant sanctuary to unwonted characteristics that would otherwise be extirpated.

CLXVIII

Having extirpated all of the base qualities for which the world once praised you and on which you used to pride yourself since they brought you power and success replace them at once with all of the noble ones you never saw any advantage to yourself in possessing and therefore neglected to cultivate.

CLXIX

Force yourself to be as perfect as you could only have been if you had never debased yourself by coming into being.

CLXX

Invent the first instrument capable of accurately measuring the distance each man has fallen from his ideal.

CLXXI

Do battle with devious concepts that defile the mind in the shadows of consciousness where they dwell.

CLXXII

Catapult yourself to a higher level of humility by heaping the sincerest praise you are capable of on the achievements of the man you hate most.

CLXXIII

Unlock the laws of a lost world system.

CLXXIV

Spin on the inaccessible apex of infinite space, as swift and volatile as a flame.

CLXXV

Master the art of remaining at rest.

CLXXVI

Complete your task in total quietude.

CLXXVII

Pray to receive less than what you will have after you have lost everything.

CLXXVIII

Foresee what the future will be like if you let events unfold without trying to influence their outcome.

CLXXIX

Bow eternally with your entire being to attainments you do not know.

CLXXX

Ask yourself if the respect the possible commands is merited.

CLXXXI

Scrupulously avoid committing any act you might have occasion to regret in the future.

CLXXXII

Make total quietude your only task.

CLXXXIII

Silently persist, unmovingly serene, in the same place, for millions of years.

CLXXXIV

By grace of the limitless compassion you feel live so many lives at once you can no longer differentiate the suffering collectively experienced by countless beings of every kind from your own.

CLXXXV

Completely extirpate the impulse toward any action that produces a less perfect result than universal joy.

CLXXXVI

Put an end to the horror of what has never happened.

CLXXXVII

After sending all of your baser impulses into permanent exile proceed to do an inestimable amount of good in every sphere of being.

CLXXXVIII

Be as protective of each thing this universe contains as if you yourself had created it.

CLXXXIX

Keep killing yourself until you're perfect.

CXC

Having never once derogated from your commitment to the impossible, die pure.

CXCI

Achieve the highest virtue, aware neither of what it is, nor that you have.

Generate Positivity

CXCII

Generate positivity in a vacuum.

CXCIII

Correctly identify, and unfailingly take, the path without beginning.

CXCIV

Walk, holding a thread of light in your hand, through a maze of revolving mirrors.

CXCV

Watch today diminish.

CXCVI

Seek to destroy what doesn't exist.

CXCVII

Live in a place the animals have left.

CXCVIII

Corrupt your solitude by rehearsing in your head a thousand conversations you'll never have.

CXCIX

Succeed in losing everything—to start with, your place in the universe.

CC

Travel at the speed of light and never arrive.

CCI

Expect the seed of impossibility to germinate in the present moment.

CCII

Let the memory of delight elude you.

CCIII

Having pried your mind free from all practical concerns at last, grant it the autonomy to perform, unmolested, its proper office of ministering to insoluble problems.

CCIV

Split the ocean into four equal parts.

CCV

Measure the distance between each drop of rain.

CCVI

Eternally pursue the incomplete.

CCVII

Unknowingly encourage misfortunes that haven't yet occurred by denying their possibility.

CCVIII

Accidentally trample your hopes into the dust before they can be blasted.

CCIX

Persist in speaking of happiness as if you possessed it.

CCX

Admire the passive wisdom of what undermines its own power.

CCXI

Live a blind marionette of immortal beings you're oblivious to.

CCXII

Blindly celebrate, by moving through the days allotted to you like a somnambulist, the fixed and inscrutable character of the destiny you've been assigned.

CCXIII

Commit yourself to projects that baffle your powers and so resist completion.

CCXIV

Attempt the impossible without trying.

CCXV

Put a one hundred and twenty year holiday between yourself and the task at hand.

CCXVI

Try harder at desiring to accomplish less.

CCXVII

Disobey the rules that hamper the derangement that feeds the deluded frenzy of useless inspiration.

CCXVIII

Make a valiant effort to confer legitimacy on what generates hope.

CCXIX

Smash headfirst into the moment to come.

CCXX

Somnolently nourish the sensation of hopelessness that arises as a result of not having a mind that can reach a state of rest in the midst of perpetual collapse.

CCXXI

Collapse in disappointment each time the impossible fails to occur.

CCXXII

Pit your material form against its reflected image in a fight to the death.

CCXXIII

Pay homage, with each of your memories, to an unknown future occurrence.

CCXXIV

Act as if surrender to what you cannot control were the equivalent of making a conscious decision.

CCXXV

Cling to the belief that if you keep asserting your will the nature of the universe will change.

CCXXVI

Appreciate the persistence of this opaque screen coextensive with the knowledge sense perception affords.

CCXXVII

Allow your illusions to take control of your life.

CCXXVIII

Admire the tranquil stillness of what has stopped working.

CCXXIX

Wait an eternity for tomorrow to come.

CCXXX

Display your mastery of passivity by standing, motionless, in the path of an avalanche.

CCXXXI

Live at the limit of hope.

CCXXXII

Become more incomplete than you can.

CCXXXIII

Unconsciously accomplish purposeless feats you consider impossible.

CCXXXIV

After a great leap forward, find yourself, once again, at the beginning.

Become a Mirror of the Universe

CCXXXV
Become a mirror of the universe and a mystery to yourself.

CCXXXVI
Live in the light that cannot be seen.

CCXXXVII
Brand an esoteric symbol of uncertain meaning into the substance of your brain.

CCXXXVIII

Vow to serve what the sky conceals.

CCXXXIX

Walk through this world without touching anything in it, not even the ground beneath your feet.

CCXL

Forget how it feels to be influenced by visible forces.

CCXLI

Celebrate the impermanence of the composite forms you recoil from.

CCXLII

Conduct a silent choir of luminescent creatures in the performance of a polyphonic mass that summons forth a procession of dazzling visions from those two portals of tenebrosity thrown open on the beyond, the pupils of a dead saint's eyes.

CCXLIII

Become aware of the arabesques being traced in your soul by the silence of God as you sleep.

CCXLIV

Accept delivery of the light capable of traversing any distance.

CCXLV

Doubt the reality of anything but purity.

CCXLVI

Refuse to be destroyed by the dangerous illusion that what you love exists.

CCXLVII

Sit beside an angel on the edge of the world.

CCXLVIII

Suffer nothing to come between yourself and the undiscerned source of the sky's vastness.

CCXLIX

Close your eyes to everything but the life to come.

CCL

Invite a being you can't perceive to confer on you a name you can't pronounce.

CCLI
Explain, with a silent look, what eludes comprehension.

CCLII
Ecstatically contemplate disassembled splendor.

CCLIII
While seeming to move in the same direction as others, arrive elsewhere.

CCLIV
Never leave this circle of light.

CCLV
Live enclosed in the silent contentment acceptance of death's certainty brings.

CCLVI

Trust in your ability to transcend all names.

CCLVII

Advance so far into the light of truth you become invisible to the world.

CCLVIII

Deliver the light capable of traversing any distance.

CCLIX

Live unknown to nature.

CCLX

Slide through the doors of time untouched.

CCLXI
Travel unmoving, traversing the universe, directionless.

CCLXII
With maniacal persistence repeat the same word until you succeed in exposing the unreality the sound of it conceals.

CCLXIII
Say the unknown name.

CCLXIV
Surround yourself with unseeable light.

CCLXV
Gaze into your mind, a mirror of the universe held in God's hand.

Reach the Heights of Joy

CCLXVI
Reach the heights of joy, ruined for good.

CCLXVII
Sleepily prophesy a future like the past which has vanished in which you will obliviously live through every lacerating moment that eludes your memory once again blissfully unaware of the number of times you have barely survived these same tribulations before.

CCLXVIII
Hold onto the light as if it were a ledge as you fall.

CCLXIX

Serenade the sun of life with the darkness of hell using a typhoon of secret craving for inescapable torment as an amplifier.

CCLXX

Experience a happiness that never happens.

CCLXXI

Explore the impossibility of a contentment that endures.

CCLXXII

Make your delight the necessary sequel of nothing that seems to deserve it.

CCLXXIII

Become entangled in troubles you can't endure for reasons you don't understand.

CCLXXIV

Climb to the top of an extinguished candle.

CCLXXV

Live on the gilded heights of the hope you have lost.

CCLXXVI

Search in darkness for what eludes discovery.

CCLXXVII

Keep your eyes closed until the light appears.

CCLXXVIII

Grind today's desires to dust against the cold granite of future regret.

CCLXXIX
Treat each day as an attack.

CCLXXX
Salute, with a blank look, another loss.

CCLXXXI
Scrape that crushed flowerlike face off the surface of the road it was flattened against.

CCLXXXII
Make a permanent exhibit of your broken heart.

CCLXXXIII
Live without relief.

CCLXXXIV

Stare blankly at the floor.

CCLXXXV

Lie in bed all morning listening to the rain.

CCLXXXVI

Without knowing why, get up and leave.

CCLXXXVII

Sail between Scylla and Charybdis on a freshly solidified sheet of lead.

CCLXXXVIII

Move sideways through impenetrable darkness for the next six thousand years.

CCLXXXIX

Accidentally destroy your ideal world.

CCXC

Do the opposite of what you intend without realizing you have until it's too late.

CCXCI

Establish the first in an indefinite series of catastrophic outcomes.

CCXCII

Unknowingly move a little further away from the future you hope for with every step you take.

CCXCIII

Compete in darkness with the self you have created for a nonexistent prize.

CCXCIV

In a cast iron skillet hung over the flames of hell boil the tears of a beast of prey.

CCXCV

Lose again what you already lost, unknowingly, before.

CCXCVI

Continue to increase the volume of your screams until you are convinced by the lack of response they provoke that if you are indeed producing sounds as you assume they are of a kind which cannot be heard.

CCXCVII

Test the idea that pain is a delusion.

CCXCVIII

Plunge down unluckily from your place in the sky.

CCXCIX
Record the history of light's collapse.

CCC
Voicing no further protest deliver your exhausted heart into the annihilating power of pure contentment.

CCCI
Lie down on a bed of nails prepared for you by an angel of hell on the crest of a collapsing wave of tears one hundred feet tall.

CCCII
Holding aloft a burned out torch, leap, eyes closed, into the abyss.

Achieve Perfection

CCCIII
Achieve perfection and vanish from the face of the earth without influencing anyone.

CCCIV
Write down all you remember of the last eight billion years.

CCCV
Become as complete as a period of silence.

CCCVI

Disdain to experience what words exist to express.

CCCVII

Understanding now there is nothing to attain and indeed never was be as imperturbably content as you should have been to begin with.

CCCVIII

Rejoice as if witness to the felicitous result of a miracle you don't remember performing.

CCCIX

Go where the waves came from.

CCCX

Be where the waves went.

CCCXI

Remain in the place where you're unperceived.

CCCXII

Move one step nearer to another world.

CCCXIII

Smile placidly into the vacant immensity of a universe unfathomable to the mind.

CCCXIV

Henceforth have nothing to do with any of the habits you have acquired.

CCCXV

Remain as calm and untroubled at all times as if you were still unborn, circumventing the turbulence of your present existence to bathe luxuriously in the serenity of the void which preceded it.

CCCXVI

Maintain your mind in a completely immaculate state at all times no matter what.

CCCXVII

Forget the name you were given.

CCCXVIII

Work miracles which go unnoticed.

CCCXIX

Practise seeing what's disappeared.

CCCXX

Always write with your own blood, regardless of whether you're transcribing a sutra, celebrating despair in a lyric, or signing a deposit slip.

CCCXXI

Die to the pleasures of a world you're unaware of.

CCCXXII

Water the plant on your windowsill with the tears of compassion shed by a bodhisattva until each of its leaves—unprecedentedly nourished—develops into an independent, self-renewing source of light.

CCCXXIII

Demonstrate characteristics increasingly similar to those of infinite space.

CCCXXIV

Push long waves of transformative love in a soothing rhythm over the lacerated surface of the world ceaselessly for centuries without number until the affliction whose consummate manifestation is human consciousness heals.

CCCXXV

Throw away everything at once.

CCCXXVI

Walk straight out of this world into the next without pausing to turn around.

CCCXXVII

Walk with feet as light as a fly's across the face of God.

CCCXXVIII

Allow your tongue to anticipate the silence that is all that will remain at the last moment.

CCCXXIX

Become as complete as a period of silence to which no term can be put.

CCCXXX

Seek permanent residence in desired imperfection.

CCCXXXI

Live without leaving a trace.

Rise Toward Heaven

CCCXXXII
Rise toward heaven on the crystalline wave of an ultratoxic tsunami of tears of inconsolable torment destined to increase in size until its sizzling crest of lethal silver pierces like the tip of a poisoned blade through the skin of an angel as resplendent as a star being borne by grace through the sky above.

CCCXXXIII
See yourself destroyed.

CCCXXXIV
See the world destroyed.

CCCXXXV
Notice nothing exists.

CCCXXXVI
Become cognizant of a dark knot of secrets hidden deep in the mind of God.

CCCXXXVII
Superimpose the horns of an antelope on the shadow of a hyena.

CCCXXXVIII
Inspired by a selfless love you despise because you're incapable of it make a false sacrifice which saves millions.

CCCXXXIX
Forget the grace you have.

CCCXL
Leave the light behind.

CCCXLI
Declare the core of the earth your personal kingdom.

CCCXLII
Each day, with the same splendid ardor, annihilate all possibility of hope.

CCCXLIII
Demand to be given everything, knowing none of it is yours.

CCCXLIV
Engineer a delay that looks like it will be brief but ends up lasting forever.

CCCXLV

Determine the truth of the matter prior to investigating.

CCCXLVI

Neglect to disclose the truth after destroying the evidence.

CCCXLVII

Lie down in the dust.

CCCXLVIII

Prostrate yourself before a bottomless pit.

CCCXLIX

Live the tortured prisoner of the judgments you have passed.

CCCL

Accidentally discover proof of the existence of the vacuum nature abhors in your heart.

CCCLI

Raise sleep to the level of a destiny.

CCCLII

Impale the severed head of your sworn foe—felled at last!—on the apex of an equilateral triangle.

CCCLIII

Having not yet received access to the nectar of the gods be content for now to quench your thirst with water contaminated by a chemical spill.

CCCLIV

Feast with Luciferian melancholy on the forgotten ruins of a fallen kingdom.

CCCLV

Hold the hopes of those who pray to you for help in hands as cold as marble.

CCCLVI

Constantly evaluate everything this universe contains from the pitiless vantage point of permanent dissatisfaction.

CCCLVII

Drive your equanimity off a cliff like an ambulance without brakes.

CCCLVIII

Announce who will die next, unaware you're the one.

CCCLIX
Conceive projects dependent on a power of illusion unsurpassed in the history of desire.

CCCLX
Let undisciplined craft monitor your progress, as unbridled imagination corrects your mistakes.

CCCLXI
Divine the mania that will prompt you tomorrow.

CCCLXII
Act the same way now as you would in a world that didn't exist.

CCCLXIII
Make the costliest mistake imaginable without a care in the world.

CCCLXIV

Unduly honor what is least deserving of commendation by decorating it with awards.

CCCLXV

Be a tomb of comfort for speechless terror.

CCCLXVI

Never propose the solution you claim to possess.

CCCLXVII

Think with blurred amazement of the man you might have been.

CCCLXVIII

With the blade of a guillotine left over from revolutionary France carve the first letter of the name of your future assassin into the fragrant bark of one of the cedars of Lebanon.

CCCLXIX

Frantically attempt to wrench your past actions free from their karmic consequences before the next blow falls.

CCCLXX

Reserve a seat for the self you have constructed on a Charonic cruise to the other side.

CCCLXXI

Like a drunken soldier cast into a Dionysian frenzy by the cacophonous music of the coming apocalypse dance at midnight in barefooted confusion through a blizzard of shrapnel down the sharp incline of mountain of shattered bone banging with an arhythmical frenzy born of feverish delirium on the black tambourine of doom.

CCCLXXII

See the idea of yourself that preceded you destroyed.

CCCLXXIII

See the idea of the world that preceded the world destroyed.

CCCLXXIV

Notice, once again, nothing exists, neither phenomenal things nor noumenal things, neither the thing with which your deceived senses deceive you in turn nor the thing-in-itself.

CCCLXXV

Don't believe this could be dust.

CCCLXXVI

Certain the truth will tear you to pieces, deny it every turn.

CCCLXXVII

Move downward relentlessly from an indefinable number of unseen places with that disregard for all precision characteristic of the rain.

CCCLXXVIII

Plant a rose garden in the core of a nuclear reactor.

CCCLXXIX

Supervise the sky's collapse.

CCCLXXX

Hallucinate the hand of an angel drawing a circle of light around a sun that's gone.

Sit in the Center of a Circle of Light

CCCLXXXI

Sit in the center of a circle of light, your eyes closed.

CCCLXXXII

Seize the essence of the sun in your outstretched hand.

CCCLXXXIII

Look on, dumbfounded, as decades of laboriously acquired knowledge disappear in a flash, miraculously unclogging the major causeways of your mind.

CCCLXXXIV

Address everyone alike with lunar delicacy—or keep, unswervingly, the silence of the dead.

CCCLXXXV

Let a beauty that transcends the material world break your heart.

CCCLXXXVI

Delay the memory of the light you see moving toward you tomorrow.

CCCLXXXVII

Cease to appear as yourself.

CCCLXXXVIII

Cease to appear to yourself as yourself.

CCCLXXXIX

Imagine what it must feel like to have four equal sides.

CCCXC

Solidify into an inconceivable form.

CCCXCI

Act as if the world were standing still.

CCCXCII

Run toward the trees.

CCCXCIII

Wherever it is you think you're going, arrive there tomorrow like the rain.

CCCXCIV
Release the soul of a trapped divinity into the forest at dawn.

CCCXCV
Lie down in stardust.

CCCXCVI
Watch the world slip away into the distance without you.

CCCXCVII
From a barely audible sermon of indecipherable subtlety you heard in a dream and feel helpless to translate into the language of men gather a few fragile yet luminous threads of moral guidance.

CCCXCVIII
Fix what the sky fell on.

CCCXCIX

Name an infinite number of forgotten worlds.

CD

Carry the last day of summer to the edge of the sea.

CDI

On the shore of a nameless island erect the statue of an unknown god.

CDII

Discern light's hidden undulations.

CDIII

Act as if purity were the only reality until it is.

CDIV

Stop and savor your fatigue in the cold silence of the incessantly falling snow of the mountain you have just ascended.

CDV

Flow with the river towards the last drop of rain.

CDVI

Delay the seasonal alarm of this harsh luminosity a few moments longer.

CDVII

Lose your way just as the mist recedes.

CDVIII

Among departed things of unperceived beauty let the universe you created in your mind while you were still alive be the first of which all memory was lost.

CDIX

Forget everything but the grace you have.

CDX

Take nothing, knowing all of it is yours.

CDXI

Aspire to die a little closer to the stars each day.

CDXII

Revert to a previous state of being it is beyond your power to imagine.

CDXIII

Take a walk sometime tomorrow twenty miles above the sky.

CDXIV

Like a wrecked vessel cut adrift languorously traverse an infinite number of uncreated worlds.

CDXV

Become too vast to comfortably exist within the narrow confines of this universe.

CDXVI

Follow in the footsteps of a ray of light that has learned to exist independently of its source.

CDXVII

Your soul having been purified of all dross by a night of insomnia twenty-seven centuries long emerge from the stilled tempest of your bed with perfect equilibrium and proclaim yourself God.

Live Another Day

CDXVIII
Live another day in defiance of natural law.

CDXIX
Die a little bit quicker than you're able to kill yourself.

CDXX
Let the last thing you remember be the name of the nearest star.

CDXXI

Write the word sleep in the snow using a withered plum blossom branch as a calligraphy brush.

CDXXII

Become a symbol of what cannot be said.

CDXXIII

Breathe in the pure mountain air, buried alive.

CDXXIV

Keep the appointment with the apocalypse which your ancestors, in their prescience, have made for you.

CDXXV

At the top of each page of your diary write the name of a dead star.

CDXXVI

Make your life into a dream you don't remember before it becomes one.

CDXXVII

Collect the candlelit faces of four hundred and seventy-two suicides consigned to oblivion in a basket of honeycomb dripping with blood before spring comes.

CDXXVIII

Imagine what you'd do next if none of this were real.

CDXXIX

With the fascinated indifference of an omniscient amnesia watch from an immeasurable distance as the mirage of what desire still pursues blindly speeds past the evaporated mist of what was never possessed except in a dream.

CDXXX

Take your leave of this world where you have lived with a love for it you have never felt.

CDXXXI

Greet, once again, everything that has gone, when it returns, the same as ever.

CDXXXII

Praise the wisdom of what has stopped.

CDXXXIII

Live another day, unaware of why.

CDXXXIV

Keep going backwards until the place you remember beginning is gone.

CDXXXV
Master implacable regret in the twelfth month.

CDXXXVI
Know what awaits you.

CDXXXVII
Know nothing awaits you.

CDXXXVIII
Let the pain you have forgotten guide you.

CDXXXIX
Cling for as long as you can to the faded memory of a face seen through the mist.

CDXL

Using a slab of unhewn marble in lieu of a mirror study your reflection.

CDXLI

Suddenly discover evidence of death everywhere you look.

CDXLII

Collapse into the light.

CDXLIII

Name the fallen waves which have risen again after the extinct stars whose light continues to shine.

CDXLIV

Pay homage to the derailment of your original aim.

CDXLV

Let your memories of this world you're about to leave float away on the summer breeze of a dying man's breath.

CDXLVI

Think about what it means to embark alone.

CDXLVII

Indefinitely postpone your departure from the place where nothing stays.

CDXLVIII

Return to the world when it's gone.

CDXLIX

Dive backwards into an ocean of dead energy.

CDL

Climb to that spherical snowstorm the mind's confusion has named the sun on an incinerated ladder of autumn leaves.

CDLI

Perceive the existence of the light that never appears.

CDLII

Escaping from the prison of your omnipresence, aspire to dwell nowhere.

CDLIII

Become as quiet as the woods, winter solstice having arrived.

CDLIV

Notice forty-four lamps in two rows thirteen feet away from each other set out along the path in the snow after nightfall.

CDLV
Return the seasons to their starting point.

CDLVI
Bring the revolutions of the earth to an abrupt stop.

CDLVII
Watch the risen waves fall and the fallen waves rise without understanding.

CDLVIII
Float away like laughter on the wind.

CDLIX
Set fire to the dust beneath your feet.

CDLX

Remember nothing but the sound of the rain.

CDLXI

Simultaneously pacify all four elements.

CDLXII

Having strained yourself to the maximum limit of your power, accomplish nothing and collapse exhausted.

CDLXIII

Tiptoe backward through limitless time toward universal bliss.

CDLXIV

Let the last remnants of the thoughts in your mind melt and fall into the trough of a wave twenty miles away.

CDLXV

Catch sight of the glittering reflection of a distant star floating on the surface of your morning coffee right before the bomb goes off, killing everyone.

CDLXVI

Return to the world when it's gone without noticing it's there.

CDLXVII

Build a bridge of water across a river of fire three thousand miles long to reach the seventy-nine lightning bolts buried in the snow like phosphorescent branches fallen from the tree of life lying on the ground before the gates of paradise.

CDLXVIII

Prove you are still in the place where you started.

CDLXIX
Fast forward to the scene where everything turns white.

CDLXX
Live another day in the light of eternity.

CDLXXI
Be the light from above which arrives at the penultimate moment to immerse in the consolatory warmth of its unforeseen radiance what little remains of the faded mirage of a world irremediably wrecked.

CDLXXII
Fugitive from birth, sleep, serene, in the cool sanctuary of the Egyptian blue shadow cast by the wing of a dragon.

www.ingramcontent.com/pod-product-compliance
Lightning Source LLC
Chambersburg PA
CBHW070110120526
44588CB00032B/1405